>•• THIS BOOK BELONGS TO ••<

....

....

....

the Secret Jungle

WRITTEN AND ILLUSTRATED BY

JESSICA COURTNEY-TICKLE

SCHOLASTIC

>• FOR ERIN AND ELSIE •<

Published in the UK by Scholastic, 2022
1 London Bridge, London, SE1 9BA
Scholastic Ireland, 89E Lagan Road, Dublin Industrial Estate, Glasnevin, Dublin, D11 HP5F

SCHOLASTIC and associated logos are trademarks and/or
registered trademarks of Scholastic Inc.

Text and illustrations © Jessica Courtney-Tickle, 2022

ISBN 978 0702 30978 6

A CIP catalogue record for this book is available from the British Library.

Printed in China
Paper made from wood grown in sustainable forests and other controlled sources.

1 3 5 7 9 10 8 6 4 2

www.scholastic.co.uk

Dusk is falling after a
busy day in the jungle. In a leafy
mangrove tree two little Borneo orangutans
YAWN and STRETCH. They have played all day,
but now it is time for bed. The jungle is awash
with sound. Insects buzz, birds chatter and
gibbons hoot and howl. Who else can
you see down on the
jungle floor?

Can you spot the Mulu flying frog? In the dark his skin turns from brown to bright green!

A pale moon emerges in the darkening sky. For some creatures on this Japanese island, the day is just beginning! The Iriomote cat and her baby climb out from their resting cave. They are hoping to catch something tasty for breakfast.

CAN YOU SEE THEIR SPOTTED MARKINGS?

Can you SEE the bright green pit viper?
He's got his eye on something ...
but something has its eye on him too!

The ruddy kingfisher has
BEAUTIFUL RED FEATHERS,
can you spot him?

Night-time has arrived
in Papua New Guinea, and with it
thousands of stars. A tree kangaroo and her
baby are trying to sleep but there is so much noise!
Great butterflies flap past, giant rats hurry through the
undergrowth squeaking loudly and — CROOOAK! A giant
Arfak river frog makes them both jump!
'KEEP IT DOWN,' the kangaroos want
to call, but they are much too sleepy.

In New Zealand the kiwi and her young hunt for insects, safe under cover of night. CAN YOU SEE THE LONG, CURVED SHAPE OF THEIR BEAKS? They have an excellent sense of smell. They can even sniff out tiny insects like woodlice!

High above in a kauri tree,
a kokako bird is watching them.
CAN YOU SPOT HIM? He has a beautiful
blue wattle, a bit
like a collar.

Night is the perfect time for the quiet jaguar and her babies to hunt for food, too. The Costa Rican jungle is cooler now, and the jaguar can see much better in the dark. Can you see what they have their eye on? A beautiful ocelot is hunting too but she won't leave her hiding place until she must, she prefers to live in secret!

CAN YOU SEE HER?

UH-OH! Who's that behind you, little turtle ...?

A sliver of light peeks over the horizon in Peru. A spider monkey is trying to get an extra five minutes of sleep, but her children are already up and want to play! Below them the river is waking up too. A large tapir is wading in for his morning swim. Further up, a capybara family are still fast asleep in the water...

CAN YOU SEE ALL SIX OF THEM?

Morning is here and the Brazilian sky is a cloudless blue. A three-toed sloth smiles at her baby as they climb VEEEERRY SLOWWWWLY from tree to tree. Can you see their long, curved claws? Baby sloth wrinkles her nose, what is that terrible smell? It can only be a stinkbird! CAN YOU SPOT HER SPIKY ORANGE HEAD?

Below them a
PINK RIVER DOLPHIN
happily rolls and dives
through the water. He
will spend most of his day
looking for the perfect
fish to eat.

The sun is high in the sky and the Rwandan jungle is getting warmer. A gorilla family are having a lazy breakfast by a stream.
CAN YOU SEE WHAT THEY ARE EATING?
One little one splashes the other and a play fight breaks out!

A bright-eyed mongoose watches them curiously. Can you count how many tiny babies she has?

A family of giraffes are eating from an acacia tree. Can you see how they stretch their long necks to pull leaves from the highest branches?

In Madagascar, breakfast has ended and a group of ring-tailed lemurs are watching the world go by. The little ones like to sit on mum's back and bury their heads in her thick fur. In another tree a red-ruffed lemur is searching for something tasty to eat!

CAN YOU SPOT SOMETHING HE MIGHT LIKE?

High above a tiny aye-aye is fast asleep in her nest. CAN YOU SEE WHERE??

IN SRI LANKA, THE MIDDAY AIR IS WARM AND HEAVY...

An elephant mother and her child are taking a much-needed drink. The rest of their herd trek SLOWLY onwards in search of a cool place to nap. It is much too hot for them to keep walking.

A TINY mouse deer is
sheltering nearby, she stares
at all the elephants in awe!

A bright kingfisher bird has
caught something tasty to eat!
CAN YOU SEE WHAT
HE'S FOUND?

Three little tiger cubs are playing with their mum.
One of them is trying to roar as loudly as he can!

RAAAAAAAAAAAAAAAAARRRRRR!

Can you see one quiet cobra who has woken with
a start? A fluffy red panda opens one eye too,
but she soon falls fast asleep again. The
heat of an Indian afternoon makes
her very sleepy!

A flying fox is ready to find a home for the night here on Christmas Island.

Her tiny baby is too little to
fly by himself yet. She hugs him
tightly to her chest and –

ONE, TWO, THREE ... WHEEEEE!

In the distance,
hundreds of red crabs are
journeying towards the ocean.

WHO ELSE CAN YOU SPOT
HEADING INTO THE WATER?

A pair of blue-footed boobies
are protecting their nest.
CAN YOU SEE HOW MANY EGGS
THEY HAVE?

The sun is sinking and another day in the jungle has come to an end.

A giant panda and her cubs are finishing their bamboo.

CAN YOU SEE WHO'S ALREADY FALLEN FAST ASLEEP?

A Pallas cat is curled up too. Soon she will wake and prowl the night looking for her first meal. We mustn't wake the pandas up – they are all snuggling down now...

GOODNIGHT, BUSY JUNGLE, SEE YOU ANOTHER DAY.

>•ORANGUTAN•<

🌿 Orangutans build a new nest to sleep in every night. In takes about ten minutes for them to pull together a simple platform made from branches. When it's raining, they'll sometimes add a roof.

🌿 Young orangutans stay with their mothers until they are about seven years old. They remain close, riding on her body and sleeping in her nest, until they have the skills to survive on their own.

🌿 Orangutans have such long arms that their fingertips nearly brush the ground when they're standing.

MORE TO SPOT: monkeys, macacques, gibbons, rhino, squirrels, slow loris, clouded leopard

>• IRIOMOTE •< CAT

🌿 These small wildcats live only on one Japanese island. Scientists think there are fewer than 150 Iriomote cats left in the wild!

🌿 Rats, frogs and fish are all on the Iriomote cat's menu. They have even been spotted swimming and diving in streams to snap up water birds.

🌿 The name for the cats in the local language is yamamaya, which means, 'cat in the mountain'.

MORE TO SPOT: crested serpent eagle, whistling green pigeon, purple heron, fireflies

>• TREE •< KANGAROO

🌿 Tree kangaroos spend most of their lives high up among the branches, munching on the leaves, flowers and ferns they find there.

🌿 Baby tree kangaroos, called joeys, stay inside a pouch on their mother's tummy for about ten months.

🌿 To escape from dangerous predators, tree kangaroos can leap all the way from the treetops to the forest floor. They can jump as far as 18 metres and hit the ground without being hurt.

MORE TO SPOT: wallaby, horseshoe bat, Victoria crowned pigeon, Raggiana bird, cassowary

>• KIWI •<

🌿 Kiwis are very odd birds – their feathers look more like fur and their plump bodies are far too heavy for flight.

🌿 Kiwis spend their lives on the ground and even burrow beneath the soil to build their nests.

🌿 Kiwis are the only birds in the world with nostrils at the end of their beaks. They use the nostrils to sniff out creepy crawlies to eat among the leaves of the forest floor.

MORE TO SPOT: New Zealand parrot, morepork owl, tomtits, red deer, possum

>• JAGUAR •<

🌿 Skilled climbers, jaguars can scramble up some of the tallest trees in their jungle homes. They use these viewpoints to keep an eye out for prey animals to pounce on below.

🌿 The black spots on jaguars' bodies are sometimes called rosettes, as they are a similar shape to roses with a black dot in the middle.

🌿 With strong teeth and powerful jaw muscles, a jaguar could bite through a turtle shell with one snap!

MORE TO SPOT: scarlet macaw, crocodile, heron, sloth, capuchin monkey, owl butterfly

>• SPIDER •<
MONKEY

🌿 When hanging upside down with their long black arms, legs and tails dangling, these monkeys look a lot like the spiders they are named after!

🌿 Like humans, spider monkeys often give each other a hug to say hello.

🌿 These clever creatures are noisy communicators! They call, whistle, bark, grunt, scream and shake trees to relay different messages.

MORE TO SPOT: red-eyed tree frog, stork, cock of the rock, harpy eagle, boa constrictor

>• SLOTH •<

🍃 Some sloths are so slow that green algae grows on their fur. The algae helps the sloths blend in among the leaves in the treetops.

🍃 As well as algae, sloths' fur makes an excellent home for lots of other living things, including moths, beetles and cockroaches.

🍃 The slowest mammal on the planet, sloths spend up to twenty hours a day sleeping! When they do decide to make a move, their top speed is around 0.2 kilometres per hour.

MORE TO SPOT: armadillo, giant otter. anteater, scarlet ibis, howler monkeys, hyacinth macaw

>• GORILLA •<

🍃 Older male gorillas are known as silverbacks, because of the silvery-grey fur that covers their backs.

🍃 These super-strong animals are thought to be at least four times more powerful than humans and can pull down a banana tree without a problem.

🍃 Gorillas are vegetarians. They eat up to 30 kilograms of fruits, leaves, grasses and other greens every day.

MORE TO SPOT: bushbuck, colobus monkey, waterbuck, tree hyrax, eagle, falls acraea butterfly

>• LEMUR •<

🍃 Ring-tailed lemurs live in groups of up to thirty animals, known as troops. The leader of the troop is usually an older female lemur.

🍃 There are more than one hundred different types of lemur, but they all live in Madagascar. The smallest is the pygmy mouse lemur, which is only about 12 centimetres long!

🍃 Some male lemurs make a stinky scent from glands in their bottoms. They rub their tails in the smell, then wave it at rivals.

MORE TO SPOT: blue vanga bird, red fody bird, silky sifake lemur, giraffe weevil, chameleon

>• ASIAN •<
ELEPHANT

- Asian elephants live in groups called herds, which are mostly made up of female family members.

- Elephant herds may travel as far as 80 kilometres per day in search of food or water.

- To keep cool in the heat of the jungle, elephants fill their trunks with water and spray it over their bodies.

- Baby elephants, called calves, sometimes suck their trunks for comfort – just like human babies sometimes suck their thumbs!

MORE TO SPOT: purple-faced langur, peacock, leaf-nosed lizard, black-necked stork, spurfowl

>• TIGER •<

- Adult tigers live alone and use scent to mark the areas they roam through, warning other tigers to stay away.

- The only big cats with stripes, tigers each have a pattern that is as unique to them as fingerprints are to us!

- Baby tigers are called cubs. They are born in litters of four to six siblings, and stay with their mother until they are about 18 months old, when they are able to hunt for themselves.

MORE TO SPOT: Indian wolf, grey langur monkeys, lime butterfly, Indian elephant, jungle fowl

>• FLYING •<
FOX

- Flying foxes are some of the largest bats in the world. During the day, they gather in big groups called camps and sleep hanging upside down.

- When flying foxes drink the tasty nectar inside flowers, pollen gets stuck to their fur. They pass the pollen between plants, helping the plants to make new seeds. This keeps the forests they live in healthy.

- On hot days, flying foxes skim over the surface of rivers and lakes, getting their tummies wet. They then lick the water off their fur.

MORE TO SPOT: blue footed boobies, manta ray, gecko, spinner dolphin, turtles, frigatebird

>• PANDA •<

- Giant pandas spend up to 16 hours a day eating! They mainly munch on a type of grass called bamboo.

- Panda cubs are born pink and furless. They are only 15 centimetres long – about the length of a teaspoon.

- Sometimes, pandas do handstands! In order to mark their scent high up a tree, they stand on their front legs, with their back legs in the air, and wee on the bark.

MORE TO SPOT: Tibetan macacque, golden snub-nosed monkey, sable, clouded leopard

Photo by Lydia Courtney-Tickle

Jessica Courtney-Tickle
is an illustrator based in Cambridge, England. She studied Illustration and Animation at Kingston University London, graduating in 2014. Jessica spends most of her time drawing for children's books, she also sells her paintings at fairs and markets across the UK.

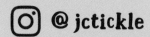 @ jctickle

>•WHAT ELSE DID •<
YOU SPOT?